DAD JOKES ON THE THRONE

Dad jokes and throne time: the perfect combination!

Welcome to "Dad Jokes on the Throne" the ultimate destination for fans of bathroom humor and dad jokes! With over 200 hilarious jokes to choose from, this book is guaranteed to keep you laughing for hours on end. Whether you're looking for a quick chuckle while you take care of business or a full-on gut-busting laughter fest, we've got you covered. Inside, you'll find a wide range of dad jokes covering everything from puns to wordplay to pure absurdity. So why wait? Grab your copy today and get ready to laugh your pants off! Whether you're in the bathroom or just looking for a good time, "Dad Jokes on the Throne" is the perfect choice.

JUST DON'T BLAME US

if you end up sitting on the throne for hours on end. these jokes are that good!

WHY WAS THE TOILET PAPER IN THE BASEMENT?

IT WAS TOO PROUD TO BE ON THE BOTTOM FLOOR.

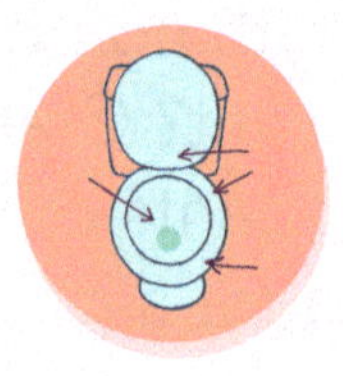

WHY COULDN'T THE BICYCLE STAND UP BY ITSELF?

BECAUSE IT WAS TWO TIRED.

WHAT DID THE TOILET SAY
TO THE TOILET BRUSH?

YOU'VE GOTTA BE KIDDING ME!

WHY WAS THE TOILET PAPER IN
THE LIVING ROOM?

IT WANTED TO WATCH TV.

WHAT DID THE TOILET SAY
TO THE OTHER TOILET?

I'LL FLUSH YOU OUT

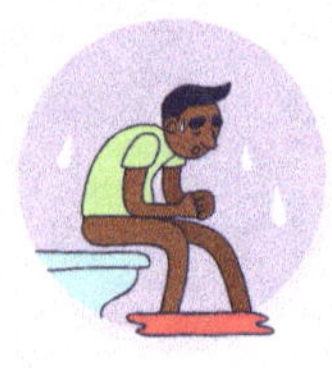

WHY WAS THE TOILET PAPER
IN THE GARDEN?

**IT WAS TOO EMBARRASSED
TO BE INSIDE.**

WHY WAS THE TOILET PAPER
IN THE KITCHEN?

IT WANTED TO BE A DISH TOWEL.

WHAT DID THE TOILET SAY
TO THE OTHER TOILET?

**YOU'RE FLUSHING MY
REPUTATION DOWN THE DRAIN.**

WHY WAS THE TOILET PAPER IN THE BEDROOM?

IT WAS FEELING A LITTLE SOFT.

WHY WAS THE TOILET PAPER IN THE ATTIC?

IT WANTED TO BE ABOVE IT ALL.

WHAT DID THE TOILET SAY TO THE OTHER TOILET?

I'LL BE A FLUSHER IF YOU'LL BE A SPITTER.

WHY WAS THE TOILET PAPER IN THE GARAGE?

IT WANTED TO BE A MECHANIC.

WHY WAS THE TOILET PAPER IN THE KITCHEN?

IT WAS FEELINGA LITTLE ROUGH.

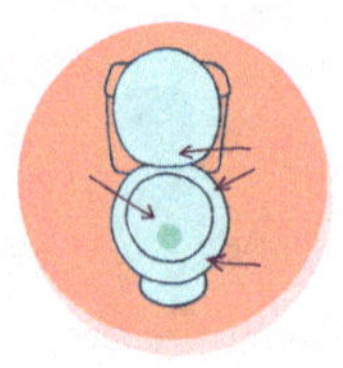

WHAT DID THE TOILET SAY TO THE OTHER TOILET?

YOU'RE FLUSHING MY SELF-ESTEEM DOWN THE DRAIN.

WHY WAS THE
TOILET PAPER IN THE BEDROOM?

IT WAS FEELING A LITTLE DIRTY.

WHY WAS THE
TOILET PAPER IN THE ATTIC?

IT WAS FEELING A LITTLE LOFT.

WHAT DID THE TOILET SAY TO THE OTHER TOILET?

I'LL FLUSH IF YOU'LL SPIT.

WHY WAS THE TOILET PAPER IN THE GARAGE?

IT WANTED TO BE A MECHANIC'S RAG.

WHY WAS THE TOILET PAPER IN THE KITCHEN?

IT WAS FEELING A LITTLE GREASY.

WHAT DID THE TOILET SAY TO THE OTHER TOILET?

YOU'RE FLUSHING MY DIGNITY DOWN THE DRAIN.

WHY WAS THE TOILET PAPER IN THE BEDROOM?

IT WAS FEELING A LITTLE SOILED.

WHY WAS THE TOILET PAPER IN THE ATTIC?

IT WAS FEELING A LITTLE DRAFTY.

WHAT DID THE TOILET SAY
TO THE OTHER TOILET?

I'LL FLUSH IF YOU'LL FLUSH TOO.

WHY WAS THE
TOILET PAPER IN THE GARAGE?

**IT WANTED TO BE
A MECHANIC'S CLOTH.**

WHY WAS THE
TOILET PAPER IN THE KITCHEN?

IT WAS FEELING A LITTLE GRIMY.

WHAT DID THE TOILET SAY
TO THE OTHER TOILET?

**YOU'RE FLUSHING
MY PRIDE DOWN THE DRAIN.**

WHY WAS THE TOILET PAPER IN THE BEDROOM?

IT WAS FEELING A LITTLE UNCLEAN.

WHY WAS THE TOILET PAPER IN THE ATTIC?

IT WAS FEELING A LITTLE DUSTY.

WHAT DID THE TOILET SAY TO THE OTHER TOILET?

I'LL FLUSH IF YOU'LL RINSE.

WHY WAS THE TOILET PAPER IN THE GARAGE?

IT WANTED TO BE A MECHANIC'S OIL RAG.

WHY WAS THE TOILET PAPER IN THE KITCHEN?

IT WAS FEELING A LITTLE GREASY.

WHAT DID THE TOILET SAY TO THE OTHER TOILET?

YOU'RE FLUSHING MY REPUTATION DOWN THE DRAIN.

WHY WAS THE TOILET PAPER IN THE BEDROOM?

IT WAS FEELING A LITTLE SOILED.

WHY WAS THE TOILET PAPER IN THE ATTIC?

IT WAS FEELING A LITTLE MUSTY.

WHY WAS THE TOILET PAPER
IN THE GARAGE?

IT WANTED TO BE A MECHANIC'S RAG.

WHY WAS THE TOILET PAPER
IN THE KITCHEN?

IT WAS FEELING A LITTLE GREASY.

WHY WAS THE MATH BOOK SAD?

IT HAD TOO MANY PROBLEMS.

WHY COULDN'T THE LEOPAR
PLAY HIDE AND SEEK?

**BECAUSE HE WAS
ALWAYS SPOTTED.**

WHY DID THE COMPUTER GET COLD?

IT LEFT ITS WINDOWS OPEN.

WHY WAS THE CAT SITTING ON THE COMPUTER?

IT WANTED TO KEEP AN EYE ON THE MOUSE.

WHY DID THE TOMATO TURN RED?

BECAUSE IT SAW THE SALAD DRESSING!

WHY DID THE COOKIE GO TO THE DOCTOR?

IT WAS FEELING CRUMBLY.

WHY DID THE SCARECROW WIN AN AWARD?

BECAUSE HE WAS OUTSTANDING IN HIS FIELD.

WHY DID THE BICYCLE FALL OVER?

BECAUSE IT WAS TWO-TIRED.

WHY COULDN'T THE BICYCLE STAND UP BY ITSELF?

IT WAS TWO-TIRED.

WHY DID THE FROG CALL HIS INSURANCE COMPANY?

HE HAD A JUMP IN HIS CAR.

WHY WAS THE CALENDAR POPULAR?

IT HAD A LOT OF DATES.

I USED TO PLAY THE VIOLIN.

NOW I JUST VIOLIN.

WHY DID THE ROBOT BREAK UP WITH HIS GIRLFRIEND?

HE COULDN'T HANDLE THE MAINTENANCE.

WHY DID THE MUSICIAN BREAK UP WITH HIS GIRLFRIEND?

SHE WAS ALWAYS HARMONIZING WITH HIM.

WHY DID THE JELLY BREAK UP WITH THE PEANUT BUTTER?

THEY JUST COULDN'T SPREAD TOGETHER.

WHY DID THE LAWYER BREAK UP WITH HIS GIRLFRIEND?

HE FOUND OUT SHE WAS SUING FOR CUSTODY OF THE BLANKET.

WHY DID THE THERAPIST BREAK UP WITH HER BOYFRIEND?

HE WAS JUST TOO CLINGY.

WHAT DID THE OCEAN SAY TO THE BEACH?

NOTHING, IT JUST WAVED.

WHY DO SEAGULLS FLY OVER THE OCEAN?

BECAUSE IF THEY FLEW OVER THE BAY, WE'D CALL THEM BAGELS.

HOW DO YOU MAKE 7 EVEN?

TAKE AWAY THE S.

WHAT CONCERT COSTS JUST 45 CENTS?

50 CENT FEATURING NICKELBACK!

I MADE A PENCIL WITH TWO ERASERS.

IT WAS POINTLESS.

WHAT DO YOU CALL A FAKE NOODLE?

AN IMPASTA.

WHERE DO MATH TEACHERS GO ON VACATION?

TIMES SQUARE.

RIP, BOILING WATER.

YOU WILL BE MIST.

I'D AVOID THE SUSHI IF I WERE YOU

IT'S A LITTLE FISHY!

MY BOSS ASKED ME WHY I ONLY GET SICK ON WORK DAYS.

I SAID IT MUST BE MY WEEKEND IMMUNE SYSTEM.

MY BOSS TOLD ME TO HAVE A GOOD DAY

SO I WENT HOME!

I JUST PAID $100 FOR A BELT THAT DOESN'T FIT

WHAT A HUGE WAIST!

WHY ARE BALLOONS SO EXPENSIVE?

INFLATION

WHY CAN'T YOU SEND
A DUCK TO SPACE?

**BECAUSE THE BILL WOULD
BE ASTRONOMICAL.**

WHAT SIDE OF A TREE GROWS
THE MOST BRANCHES?

THE OUTSIDE!

WHY DID AN OLD MAN FALL IN A WELL?

BECAUSE HE COULDN'T SEE THAT WELL!

WHAT DO YOU CALL A FISH WITH NO EYE?

A FSH.

WHY ARE ELEVATOR JOKES SO GOOD?

THEY WORK ON MANY LEVELS.

WHY DID THE COMPUTER GET MAD AT THE PRINTER?

BECAUSE IT DIDN'T LIKE ITS TONER VOICE.

WHEN DOES A REGULAR JOKE BECOME A "DAD JOKE?"

WHEN IT BECOMES APPARENT.

WHY DO BEES HAVE STICKY HAIR?

BECAUSE THEY USE A HONEYCOMB.

I'M AFRAID FOR THE CALENDAR.

ITs DAYs ARE NUMBERED.

I ONCE GOT FIRED FROM
A CANNED JUICE COMPANY.

APPARENTLY I COULDN'T CONCENTRATE.

WHAT DO SNAKES LIKE TO STUDY IN SCHOOL?

HISSSS-TORY!

WHY DID THE VEGETABLE CALL THE PLUMBER?

IT HAD A LEEK.

WHAT DO YOU CALL A DOG THAT CAN TELL TIME?

A WATCH DOG!

WHAT DO YOU CALL A COW WITH TWO LEGS?

LEAN BEEF.

WHAT'S THE BEST AIR TO BREATHE IF YOU WANT TO BE RICH?

MILLIONAIRE.

WHY DID THE GIRL TOSS A CLOCK OUT THE WINDOW?

SHE WANTED TO SEE TIME FLY.

WHAT DID ONE PLATE SAY TO ANOTHER PLATE?

TONIGHT, DINNER'S ON ME.

DID YOU HEAR ABOUT THE KING THAT WENT TO THE DENTIST?

HE NEEDED TO GET CROWNS.

WHAT HAPPENS WHEN DOCTORS GET FRUSTRATED?

THEY LOSE THEIR PATIENTS.

WHAT DO YOU CALL A BEAR WITH NO TEETH?

A GUMMY BEAR.

WHAT'S ORANGE AND SOUNDS LIKE A PARROT?

A CARROT.

WHY DID THE COACH GO TO THE BANK?

TO GET HIS QUARTER BACK.

WHAT KIND OF JEWELRY DO RABBITS WEAR?

14 CARROT GOLD.

HOW DO CELEBRITIES KEEP COOL?

THEY HAVE MANY FANS.

WHY DID THE OREO GO TO THE DENTIST?

IT LOST ITS FILLING.

HOW DO YOU GET AN ASTRONAUT'S BABY TO STOP CRYING?

YOU ROCKET.

WHY ARE FISH SO SMART?

BECAUSE THEY SWIM IN SCHOOLS.

WHAT DID ONE WALL SAY TO THE OTHER?

I'LL MEET YOU AT THE CORNER.

WHY DID THE BANANA GO TO THE DOCTOR?

BECAUSE IT WASN'T PEELING WELL.

WHERE DOES A SHEEP GO TO GET A HAIRCUT?

THE BAA BAA SHOP.

WHAT IS A CALENDAR'S FAVORITE FOOD?

DATES.

WHAT DID THE BLANKET SAY TO THE BED?

I'VE GOT YOU COVERED.

WHAT DID ONE PIECE OF TAPE SAY TO THE OTHER?

LET'S STICK TOGETHER.

WHAT DO YOU CALL A SHOE MADE OUT OF A BANANA?

A SLIPPER.

CAN FEBRUARY MARCH?

NO, BUT APRIL MAY!

WHERE DO YOU LEARN
TO MAKE ICE CREAM?

SUNDAE SCHOOL.

HOW DO YOU GET
A MOUSE TO SMILE?

SAY "CHEESE."

WHY DID THE SNOWMAN BUY
A BAG OF CARROTS?

HE WANTED TO PICK HIS NOSE.

HOW DO YOU KNOW WHEN A BIKE IS THINKING?

YOU CAN SEE ITS WHEELS TURNING.

WHAT DID ONE LEAF SAY TO THE OTHER?

I'M FALLING FOR YOU.

WHAT DO LAWYERS WEAR
TO WORK?

LAW SUITS.

WHY WAS THE TRAFFIC LIGHT
LATE TO WORK?

IT TOOK TOO LONG TO CHANGE.

I HAVE A FEAR OF ELEVATORS,

BUT I'VE STARTED TAKING STEPS TO AVOID IT.

I WAS ADDICTED TO SOAP,

BUT I'M CLEAN NOW.

WHAT DO YOU CALL A FISH WEARING A BOWTIE?

SO-FISH-TICATED.

MY DAD TOLD ME A JOKE ABOUT BOXING.

I GUESS I MISSED THE PUNCH LINE.

WHAT DO YOU CALL A MAN WITH A RUBBER TOE?

ROBERTO.

WHAT DOES A LEMON SAY WHEN IT ANSWERS THE PHONE?

"YELLOW!"

HOW DO YOU MAKE
LADY GAGA MAD?

POKE HER FACE.

WHAT DOES A HOUSE WEAR
TO A BIRTHDAY PARTY?

ADDRESS.

WHY DO SOME COUPLES GO TO THE GYM?

BECAUSE THEY WANT THEIR RELATIONSHIP TO WORK OUT.

WHAT DO YOU CALL A BELT MADE OF WATCHES?

A WAIST OF TIME.

WHAT DO YOU CALL
A HOT DOG ON WHEELS?

FAST FOOD!

WHY ARE TOILETS ALWAYS
SO GOOD AT POKER?

THEY ALWAYS GET A FLUSH

WHY DON'T EGGS TELL JOKES?

BECAUSE THEY'D CRACK EACH OTHER UP.

WHY WAS CINDERELLA THROWN OFF THE FOOTBALL TEAM?

SHE RAN AWAY FROM THE BALL.

WHY IS 6 SCARED OF 7?

BECAUSE 7 ATE 9 AND 10!

WHAT DO YOU CALL
A FLY WITHOUT WINGS?

A WALK.

DID YOU HEAR ABOUT THE ITALIAN CHEF THAT DIED?

HE PASTA WAY.

WHY DID THE COFFEE FILE A POLICE REPORT?

IT GOT MUGGED.

DID YOU HEAR ABOUT THE KIDNAPPING AT SCHOOL?

IT'S FINE, HE WOKE UP.

WHAT DID THE CLOCK DO WHEN IT WAS HUNGRY?

IT WENT BACK FOUR SECONDS.

WHAT DID THE FRIED RICE SAY TO THE SHRIMP?

DON'T WOK AWAY FROM ME!

WHY DIDN'T THE ASTRONAUT COME HOME TO HIS WIFE?

HE NEEDED HIS SPACE!

WHAT DO CLOUDS WEAR?

THUNDERWEAR.

MOM ASKED ME TO PUT KETCHUP ON THE GROCERY LIST.

NOW I CAN'T SEE ANYTHING.

DAD, CAN YOU PUT MY SHOES ON?

NO, I DON'T THINK THEY'LL FIT ME.

WHAT'S HARDER TO CATCH THE FASTER YOU RUN?

YOUR BREATH.

WHY DID THE MEXICAN
TAKE MEDS?

FOR HISPANIC ATTACKS.

BRUCE LEE WAS PRETTY FAST
BUT HIS BROTHER

SUDDEN LEE WAS EVEN FASTER.

WHY DID THE PHOTOGRAPH GO TO PRISON?

IT WAS FRAMED.

WHY CAN'T A HORSE STAND ON AN ELEPHANT'S BACK?

BECAUSE IT ISN'T THAT STABLE.

WHICH TREES HAVE THE
MOST FRIENDS?

POPLAR TREES.

I HAVE A BUNCH OF JOKES ABOUT
UNEMPLOYED PEOPLE

SADLY, NONE OF THEM WORK.

WHAT IS IT CALLED WHEN
TWO CELEBRITIES ARE FIGHTING?

STAR WARS.

I LOST MY WIFE'S AUDIOBOOK

**AND NOW I'LL NEVER HEAR
THE END OF IT!**

LEFT MY JOB AT
THE CHEMICAL FACTORY

IT WAS A TOXIC WORKPLACE

WHAT DO YOU CALL A ZOMBIE
WHO DOESN'T JOKE AROUND?

DEAD SERIOUS.

AN ONION JUST TOLD ME A JOKE

I DON'T KNOW WHETHER TO LAUGH OR CRY

WAS GOING TO MAKE A JOKE ABOUT SODIUM

BUT THEN I THOUGHT NA

COSMETIC SURGERY USED TO BE SUCH A TABOO SUBJECT

NOW YOU CAN FREELY TALK ABOUT BOTOX AND NOBODY RAISES AN EYEBROW

I'VE JUST FINISHED READING A BOOK ABOUT A BANK VAULT.

IT WAS QUITE HARD TO GET INTO.

WHAT DO YOU CALL TWO MONKEYS WHO SHARE AN AMAZON ACCOUNT

PRIME MATES

WHERE DO BOATS GO WHEN THEY'RE SICK?

TO THE DOCK.

I ASKED 10 PEOPLE WHAT LGTBQ STANDED FOR

COULDN'T GET A STRAIGHT ANSWER!

WHAT IS THE SCARIEST TREE?

BAMBOO!

WHO IS THE MOST LONELY BILLIONAIRE?

ALONE MUSK.

PEOPLE ARE USUALLY SHOCKED WHEN THEY FIND OUT

I'M A BAD ELECTRICIAN.

WHERE DO YOU FIND A COW WITH NO LEGS?

WHEREVER YOU LEFT IT.

I HAD A GREAT JOKE ABOUT COVID

BUT I DON'T WANNA SPREAD IT AROUND.

WHAT DO YOU CALL A MOM WHO TURNS INTO A DAD?

TRANSPARENT

TO THE PERSON WHO STOLE MY PLACE IN THE QUEUE.

I'M AFTER YOU NOW.

DOCTOR: I THINK YOUR DNA IS BACKWARDS.

ME: ...AND?

WHY ARE SPIDERS SO SMART?

THEY CAN FIND EVERYTHING ON THE WEB.

WHAT DO YOU CALL
A HIPPIE'S WIFE?

MISSISSIPPI.

WHY IS THE LETTER A
LIKE A FLOWER?

BECAUSE A "B" COMES AFTER IT!

THE GUY WHO STOLE MY DIARY DIED YESTERDAY.

MY THOUGHTS ARE WITH HIS FAMILY.

WHAT'S THE EASIEST WAY TO BURN 1000 CALORIES?

LEAVE THE PIZZA IN THE OVEN.

WHEN TWO VEGANS GET IN AN ARGUMENT,

IS IT STILL CALLED A BEEF?

WHAT'S A HORSE'S NUMBER ONE PRIORITY WHEN VOTING?

THE STABLE ECONOMY!

MY PRINTER'S NAME IS
BOB MARLEY.

BECAUSE IT'S ALWAYS JAMMIN'.

WHAT'S A COMPUTER'S
FAVORITE SNACK?

MICROCHIPS!

MY WIFE SAID IF I BOUGHT HER A STUPID GIFT, SHE WOULD BURN IT.

SO I BOUGHT HER A CANDLE.

WHAT WOULD THE TERMINATOR BE CALLED IN HIS RETIREMENT?

THE EXTERMINATOR.

WHAT DID ONE HAT SAY
TO THE OTHER?

STAY HERE! I'M GOING ON AHEAD.

THE BEST GIFT I EVER RECEIVED
WAS A BROKEN DRUM.

YOU CAN'T BEAT THAT.

WHAT KIND OF TEA IS HARD TO SWALLOW?

REALITY

WHAT DO YOU CALL A SAD STRAWBERRY?

A BLUE STRAWBERRY.

WHERE DID THE CAT GO AFTER LOSING ITS TAIL?

TO THE RETAIL STORE.

IF APPLE MADE A CAR,

WOULD IT HAVE WINDOWS?

WHAT'S THE OPPOSITE OF ARTIFICIAL INTELLIGENCE?

NATURAL STUPIDITY.

WHAT DO YOU CALL A CAN OPENER THAT DOESN'T WORK?

A CAN'T OPENER.

WHAT'S AN ASTRONAUT'S FAVORITE CANDY?

A MARS BAR.

WHY DID THE BULLET END UP LOSING HIS JOB?

HE GOT FIRED.

WHAT DO SKATEBOARDERS DO WHEN THEY ARE REALLY GOOD?

THEY GOPRO.

WHAT DO YOU GET FROM A PAMPERED COW?

SPOILED MILK.

HOW DOES A COMPUTER GET DRUNK?

IT TAKES SCREENSHOTS.

WHAT SHOULD YOU GIVE A SOCCER PLAYER ON HIS BIRTHDAY?

A RED CARD.

DAD WHAT ARE CLOUDS MADE OF?

LINUX SERVERS, MOSTLY.

WHAT DID 0 SAY TO 8?

NICE BELT.

DO RACING DRIVERS EVER STOP DURING A RACE?

YES, WHEN THEY ARE GETTING TIRED.

WHAT DO YOU CALL A JUNE BUG IN SEPTEMBER?

A SURVIVOR.

WHAT DID BABY CORN SAY TO MAMA CORN?

WHERE'S POP CORN?

I DON'T TRUST STAIRS.

THEY'RE ALWAYS UP TO SOMETHING.

WHAT DO YOU CALL SOMEONE WITH NO BODY AND NO NOSE?

NOBODY KNOWS.

WHAT KIND OF CAR DOES AN EGG DRIVE?

A YOLKSWAGEN.

WHY WAS THE SMARTPHONE FEELING DEPRESSED?

BECAUSE IT HAD TOO MANY "LOW BATTERY" MOMENTS!

WHY WAS THE COMPUTER HUNGRY?

IT FORGOT TO "LOG OFF" AND MISSED DINNER!

WHY DID THE SMARTPHONE GET INTO TROUBLE?

IT WAS CAUGHT "PHISHING" FOR PERSONAL INFORMATION!

WHY WAS THE COMPUTER A BAD LIAR?

IT COULDN'T KEEP A "STRAIGHT FACE" ONLINE!

WHY WAS THE COMPUTER ALWAYS SO ORGANIZED?

IT HAD A LOT OF "FOLDERS"!

WHY WAS THE KITCHEN ALWAYS SO CLEAN?

IT HAD A LOT OF "APPLIANCES"!

WHY DO DAD JOKES
ALWAYS GET A BAD RAP?

THEY'RE "CORNY"!

WHY WAS THE KID'S BEDROOM
ALWAYS SO MESSY?

BECAUSE IT WAS FULL OF "TOYS"!

DAD JOKES ON THE THRONE

Dad jokes and throne time: the perfect combination!

Thank you for purchasing "Dad Jokes on the Throne"! We hope that you've had as much fun reading these jokes as we did collecting them. Remember, sharing is caring – so be sure to pass this book along to a friend or family member who could use a good laugh. And if you're feeling generous, you could even buy a second copy for the ultimate throne room library.

THANKS AGAIN FOR YOUR SUPPORT, AND HAPPY JOKING!

www.ingramcontent.com/pod-product-compliance
Lightning Source LLC
La Vergne TN
LVHW010356160826
845677LV00005BA/1295

* 9 7 9 8 3 7 2 6 8 2 8 6 3 *